Advance Praise for *hood criatura*

"féi iká shumarí's first collection is a masterpiece of intersectionality, not only showing the bridges between identities but the necessary focal point of that project: understanding a fuller self that is available to the world. Unlike other poets who lose themselves in the writing of identity and feel at odds with their many parts, iká shumarí finds themself by imagining new worlds and deeper realities where all the pieces of a person are allowed to exist together. Through the journeys of origin, family, culture, race, language, magic, the working-poor, gender, sexuality, immigration, the hood, loss, and love shumari's collection speaks to the new poetics of the 21st century, what I call 'poetics of the radical imagination.' *Hood Criatura* functions as both a dare and an invitation, asking readers to imagine more through being whole. An important, timely work from an emerging QTPOC voice that should be on every shelf."
–Meliza Bañales, Lambda Finalist 2016, author *Life Is Wonderful, People Are Terrific*

"*Hood Criatura* by féi iká shumarí is an absorbing, big-hearted, beautiful collection. These poems of belonging, of being of many worlds at once, made me laugh with joy even as they consoled me through their sorrows, which are our sorrows, our collective experiences. Formally complex, with a gifted ear for languages, féi iká shumarí's poetry presents an important, bursting voice. These poems speak to the undocumented experience, the trans experience, and the human experience as observed by a deeply perceptive mind."
–Kali Fajardo-Anstine, National Book Award Finalist and author of *Sabrina & Corina*

"féi iká shumarí's poems expand and contract like breath—inhaling and exhaling. Making you realize what you hold in your hands is a breathing creature. First, you must stare at them, looking before you leap into the words, and then you read them aloud, letting them inhabit your voice, which, all on its own, will recite back to you a trippy Chihuahua-Inglewood hoodrat feathered-serpent dream."
–Richard Villegas Jr., author of *I (Heart) Babylon, Tenochitlan,* and *Ysteléi & La Música Romántica*

"Whether it be in these times of brutal civil unrest or hopeful future times of peace and empathy: féi iká shumarí—a necessary narrative amplifying the voice of the trans non-binary body, the immigrant, the son, the daughter, the lover. Amplifying the voice of 'I Just Want To Belong to an America That Doesn't See Me. A Body That Defies Me. A Lover Singing Sweetly.' You cannot leave this book without being rustled, heartstormed, and inspired."
–Arianna Basco, author of *Palms Up*

"féi iká shumarí can capture the complicated relationship between being queer and brown. Their words are a rapture in our culture; they dig a breathing hole for queer nonbinary folk to exist and thrive. In this collection, they make space to be seen, felt, and heard. fei's poems exist for those of us who come from places where there is no language to speak of our magic. They permit us to celebrate all the things this country has rejected, the immigrant, the poor and the queer. Let this collection be a manifesto for those queer brown hood kids who forged their own path to exist."
–Yosimar Reyes, playwright of *Prieto*

hood
criatura

Sundress Publications • Knoxville, TN

Copyright © 2020 by féi iká shumarí
ISBN: 978-1-951979-08-9
Library of Congress Control Number: 2020938673
Published by Sundress Publications
www.sundresspublications.com

Editor: Erin Elizabeth Smith
Editorial Assistant: Anna Black
Editorial Interns: Quinn Carver Johnson, Natalie Metropulos, Ada Wofford
Colophon: Display set in Amador, text set in Sitka
Cover Design: Kristen Ton
Cover Art: "hood criatura" by féi iká shumarí
Author Photo Credit: Natalia Fonseca
Book Design: Tierney Bailey

hood criatura

féi iká shumarí

Acknowledgements

Thank you to the following anthologies and journals who saw my poems and prose as valuable additions to their compilations. Earlier renditions of my work appeared in:

The Breakbeat Poets Vol. 4: LatiNext: "Reason Men Build Walls"

Frontier Poetry: "Retrato in Names"

Hayden's Ferry Review: "Lala the Origin"

The Latinx Poetry Project: "Blistering Feet, Under Blistering Sun" and "Dressing Myself Mami"

LiveWire: "Blistering Feet, Under Blistering Sun"

NPR's *Code Switch*: "Feathered Serpiente"

Oxford Review of Books: "(resident)(illegal)/(trans)(American)/(hood)(non-binary)"

PANK Magazine: "Ángel de la Guardia"

POETRY Magazine: "Reason Men Build Walls"

Thank you to Sundress Publications for supporting and trusting my decolonial vision of the world.

Contents

Los

      quiero hasta el

           cielo del casino

                       *

             Les dedico este documento que grita,

                    que se hace bolita, y luego canta.

                      This passport is a permission,

                            a marker of existence

                 It is a dedication to all my people.

            We have always been a possibility

        even when our bodies

      didn't make it,

our spirits did.

      These gold,

        hot-cheetoh-stained papeles

            offer anyone that has never had a home,

                 a place to kiket,

             a nation to call their own.

                   This is a chubby welcome

             to the house of raritos,

        of loud ass enigmas,

of magical potentialities that were never meant to fit in.

      Let our big teeth

        cross our face be

           proof that we thrive(d).

In loving memory of
Marcela Patricia Fonseca,
Victor Ivan Lorenzana,
&
Sandra Duran Lorenzana

Before Being Flung on the Telephone Wire

god don't give a fuck about me.
she doesn't care that in this poem

red vans symbolize my uterus.
she still hurls them onto the telephone wire.

when people ask me where i'm from i say a black
line shooting through a blue sky.

my womb is a plastic bag stuck on the telephone wire—
the breeze don't change direction where i'm from, so I stay stuck.

god can be in a long white robe, crop top
and sagging jeans, or be a naked coatlicue reincarnate,

but she still don't give a fuck that my womb
is the knot where both shoes meet.

she doesn't care i'll cling between earth and blue
without a ladder tall enough to reach me.

i grew up here, on the fine line between man
and woman, penis and translucent womb.

i am a symbol that marks the dead, a tombstone
made of vans that don't bleed just hang.

this crucifixion is god's divine elaborate joke
for bodies like mine: always at war with themselves.

just toss them in the air and see what they do.
she grips her stomach, points at me and laughs.

she wants people to see me nails in palms so
they can see themselves too. see the black line

between sky and dirt, man and woman,
that keeps us in this dance of two.

i am what she envisages, my palms and feet nailed to a cross; a mirage
showing the world we're all mid-flight somewhere, heading to our destination.

Blistering Feet, Under Blistering Sun

The United States is the only gardener I know without a back
bone. Picked immigrants, planted them in

farms or white people homes or restaurants
or factories or buses or macdonal

where their Brown and Black hands
lifted the economy from depression.

Picking, growing, cleaning, scrubbing,
rotting, rearing, cooking for you! Yet y'all call us illegal?

When mami and I immigrated to this   country
she taught me little things were big things—

the garage where concrete floor was bed was actually
a mansion of imagination where mami was also my   father

where Spanish was the Bible that erased all struggle &
the nine digits branding me citizen were   non-existent.

I've always been oblivious to my blue skin or third eye,
the alien people saw in me,

until opportunities were   blank   like the social security
number I couldn't fill in   never turned in

like my vote in an election.
But before my rage lit a match and set a nation on fire mami said:

Ten paciencia, it's the spirit's way, My Sky.
Growing up mami never let my bare feet touch   ground.

She knew client's friend's whose brothers or sister's
daughters, or cousin's friends who

died with blistering feet, under a blistering
sun crossing the border. Mami taught me how to swim.

It was her way of erasing the bitter taste of dead bodies from tongue—
they call us immigrants   wetbacks   because my people never

lifted from the pits of the Rio Grande or any body of water.
Fabis speak up! Talk louder, Little Son!

She didn't want my voice to recede to the sound of a whisper
or become silent like a statistic in a middle school textbook.

Mami yelled at me and flung a finger to my face & said,
In your body one body all can stand!

&   yes   ma
they do!

                                                                              & we ain't
                                                                        going anywhere.

                                   We ain't going anywhere!

                    WE.   AIN'T.   GOING.   ANYWHERE.

Mexican Curiós

you are not a rarity of the polished sort
the kind found under a coral garden off a southern
coast in the americas auctioned and sold off in glass,
you are of the unusual fragrance, smell of burned amate

bark in temples after the massacre. you are the deep stare and pink perfume flowing between
sweaty brown boy legs who shout for balls in soccer fields. you're double
dutch on black top and faggot, sometimes him-c'mere-the-gay-boy-that-eats-hot-
cheetohs-and-is-always-with-the-girls.

      you're the kind of boy that is in everyone's chips, acting like you're from here,
but you weren't even born in centinela hospital. what dirt are you from?
      My Little Son you are a mexican curiós,
always out of place and no one will know what mud you sprout from or

what land you'll dig your tiny feet into next, so little beast, sway your hip to the drumming
pulse of wild grass by the beach, look at the beautiful beach, we made it, mami said, all in spanish.

19

dontcomeformyhood

illfuckyourshitupeventhoughihaveneverfoughtbeforeinglewoodisnotahoodhesayssideeyesandsaysits
nothinglikehishoodhesplayingolympicoppressionbutdontknowjackshitabouthowthiscityoperatesh
owrichblacknessmadeithowimmigrantssleephereandbuildsmallsquarehousesandhidehowalotofthe
mstilldontgotpapershoweveryoneherelearnedeachotherslanguagewhatdoesyourlightskintassknow
aboutshitwhenyouonlyknowyourmexicancentrichoodandarefuckenantiblackgetthefuckouttaherei
nglewoodinitsthriveinitsunreachablesilenceandshadowspassingbyatnightwegetbywehaveandyoure
nottheonlyonetocomeformemaybeitsthesoftnessthatinglewoodallowedinmetobloomaswellthatp
eoplefeeltheycanpolicehowitalkwithmyhandsorgointospanishtohideorgointoproperenglishtopre
ventmydeportationorhowidropmyjawandentermyvoicemyfirstlearnedvoicewhichsoundslikethetraffi
conarborvitaeandtheblowingwindoninglewoodaveandthebustandbuckletofmyblackandbrownandi
mmigrantkinlearningtoweaveablanketsandwefuckeachotheroverbutweworkingonitwhilewaitingin
linetogetheratthedmvbutalsosidenotenoteveniwhogrewuphereknowsthereallydarkshitbutwhatidok
nowisthatmybestfriendsdadisinjailandhisbabybrothergotshotthreetimesbutthatsnotevenmystorytot
ellbecauseletmetellyouivealwaysjuststayedhiddenbecauseididntwanttogetdeportedandmysoftassc
ouldntgetwrappedupinanythingcustherewastoomuchatstakeandineverhadabackboneanywaysbutth
atsbeyondthepointdontcomeformyhooditsnotaboutcomparingwhoshoodismoreoppressedweallcarr
yingasilentwarwhenwewalkdownalleysbutwedontaintneverhadshittoprovebuthaveyouthoughtabo
utyourlightskinnessandyourpositionalityandhowyoucomingoffrightnowandbeggingformystoryb
ymakingmedoalltheemotionallaborofyourerroniousaccusationmypreferenceinthisconversationisf
oryoutoleavemethefuckalonethereforegetthefuckouttamyfacewithyourbullshitassinterrogationido
ntoweyouanexplanationho

(resident) (illegal) /
(trans) (American) /
(hood) (non-binary)

After José Olivarez's "(Citizen)(Illegal)"

Mexican woman (illegal) and Mexican boy (illegal)
arrive to Inglewood (hood) from Mexico (illegal) and meet

American (Black) culture. Mexican woman (illegal)
scrubs toilets for rich white women (American) with her Mexican (illegal)

brown hands, while Mexican boy (illegal) learns African American Vernacular
(Black)(American) in a public school (hood). Does accepting their "alien"

status make Mexican woman (illegal) and Mexican boy (illegal) more American (citizen)?
If the boy doesn't remember the old country and claims Inglewood (Black)(hood) his country

does that make him more citizen (American)? If the Mexican woman forgets her baby's daddy and her
native country is she more American (citizen) than Mexican (illegal)? If both

the Mexican woman and the Mexican boy are light skint (white), yet undocumented (illegal), are they
more safe (American)? If Mexican woman (illegal) and Mexican boy (illegal) steal

what they can't afford from K-Mart or Sav-On should they be criminalized (illegal) for their survival?
What can the Mexican woman (illegal) and the Mexican boy (illegal) do to pursue their

American Dream without persecution or deportation (illegal), if anything at all?

In the face of immigration officer Mexican woman speaks in broken English (illegal). USCIS agent (white) looks at her passport (Mexican) and looks back at her (white). Then looks at the

Mexican boy (illegal) fluent in English (American) and looks down at his passport (Mexican), then at him again (white). The USCIS agent (white) looks at the Mexican woman's

newly wed husband (Mexican)(citizen). USCIS agent (white) looks at the husband's passport (American). If the USCIS agent (white) doesn't believe their marriage will ICE take them away

(illegal)? If the USCIS agent (white) signs the immigration packets are the Mexican woman (illegal) and the Mexican boy (illegal) safe (American)(citizen)?

If Mexican woman (illegal) and Mexican boy (illegal) get their residency (American)
should they celebrate? What happens to the trauma of being undocumented (illegal) after their

green cards (American) arrive? If they didn't need a translator to communicate with the USCIS agent are they more worthy of citizenship (American)?

If the Mexican boy uses phrases like, *check yo privilege* or *the intersections of race, gender, class, and sexuality* did he make Mexican woman's (resident)

American Dream come true (American)? If the first thought the Mexican boy (resident) has waking up is slurping men and not finishing his thesis did he fail at being American (citizen)? If his only

concern is graduating from an oppressive Liberal Arts college education (American) not made for him (hood)(illegal), is Mexican Boy less American for not assimilating to academia (citizen).

If Mexican boy learns the word "queer," struggles with: his sexuality, presenting his thesis in a symposium (American), and getting consumed with his post traumatic stress disorder (American)

is he more American (citizen) and less undocumented (illegal)? If drinking doesn't help erase the trauma is he more undocumeted (illegal) than American (citizen)?

If the Mexican boy (resident) carries his green card (American) wherever he goes, does he feel safe to travel from one state to the next (illegal)? If Mexican boy decides to write poetry in

English (American) yet is fluent in Spanish (illegal) has he picked a nation?

Mexican woman becomes a legal citizen (American), while the Mexican boy (resident)(illegal) is in college. If she still speaks English with a molasses thick accent (illegal) is she more

undocumented (illegal) than American (citizen)? Meanwhile Mexican boy chooses to not file for citizenship (American) after getting his residency (American) and protests with a communist

party (illegal). Is Mexican boy scared to not be enough American (citizen) and not enough undocumented (illegal)? What is he scared of losing or gaining?

Mexican woman has a promising business in Inglewood (Black)(hood). Mexican woman (citizen) tells Mexican boy to apply for citizenship to be protected in the face of the government (American),

because Mexican boy (resident)(illegal) is not safe. If the Mexican boy (resident) ignores Mexican woman (citizen) does he not honor her sacrifice?

or is he rebelling against a whole country (American)(white)? Mexican boy (resident)(illegal) graduates college (American) and becomes a full-time creative writing and art teacher (American)

in Inglewood (hood). If Mexican boy's (resident)(illegal) students (hood)(Black)(Mexican) call him racist towards white people (American) what should he respond? Mexican boy (resident) comes

out a third time (American). How does Mexican boy (resident)(illegal) explain that although he's very masculine presenting he's a Mexican woman (illegal). If outwardly Mexican boy is not a

boy or a girl, but the line in-between (non-binary), is he, I mean she, I mean they, not trans enough (queer)? If Mexican woman accepts Mexican trans as her child, is she more

American (citizen) than Mexican (illegal), or is she more undocumented (illegal) and unworthy of her citizenship (American)? If Mexican trans keeps their beard (non-binary), but wears

Mexican woman's blouses (queer) are they lying about about being "trans" (American)? If Mexican trans (hood)(non-binary) is scared to strut the night streets of Inglewood (hood) in heels

is Mexican trans more American (citizen) than resident (illegal)? Or are they not "hood" enough (white)? Are they stuck in limbo between borders within and outside of them (non-binary)?

If Mexican trans doesn't celebrate their passed Citizenship test (American) is it because they'll always feel like a resident (illegal),

mitigating their American culture (Black)(hood) and their trans (American)(non-binary) identity and their light skint (white) self only to never feel enough (American)(citizen)?

Ms. Flowers

Her fullest smile welcomed me to my first kindergarten class in Inglewood.
She pushed
a language not of her own through the keys of her spine
to give me a country. A Black woman showed me how to build a pyramid

out of pain and letters—I mean, wooden blocks—and call it mine,
because she knew I came from a family who did not know English
or how to own something, especially the body, I mean citizenship. Ms. Flowers
walked me into the ring of quiet children who didn't know me,

but who recognized themselves in me. They opened
their small world and said welcome to the planet. She said, *You exist too little one, sing with us*
the song of freedom, but I didn't understand English, yet I felt that through her full
lips she actually said *Te amo, tu estas protegido aquí.* Her cocoa butter skin held my little

ashy Brown hand as I cried and she said *This is your wealth* and pointed to my heart,
asked *Ya comiste?* in English and when I nodded she said *You're perfect* in Spanish.
Ms. Flowers
winked at my abuelita biting her nails behind the classroom

door window. Abuelita wanted to squeeze herself
inside the room, abort this assimilation, and deport our dreams back to the old country,
but Ms.Flowers smiled at her from afar, gave her the license to breath in The Dream,
this new country of strangers, or family, because she knew we couldn't go back.

first real nation of nations

mami's business beaming
with people, wearing all kindsa

bright yellows and greens, bustling
with song, their voices filling

every crux of stillness assumed
in a tax office. some clientes sounded

like a colibri's whisper, others had crows
in their cackle. some smacked

gum, jaw all sideways, while others eye-rolled cus they was
bougie, had a house in inglewood—they was one of those—

but we still aspired to be them, no shade.
some had just landed off a plane,

walked or kicked dirt, rode a mountain bike, or swam to make it to
532 w. arbor vitae street, inglewood, california, 90301

where my body, from my toes to my clavicle, was full
of rich music under fluorescent strips of light.

where mami, hair like light, hands of sololoy, was an angel
incarnated into an immigrant woman sitting on a throne of leather,

was a goddess of first class, was everyone's mother.
Lorenzana Services, where everyone bowed in her presence

admired the way she typed
old keys faster than a bullet, untethered,

where mami was the president
of all things IRS and filling out forms with millions of tiny empty boxes,

of chisme, who talked with hands tossed in the air and laughter when she couldn't
speak english.

mami is the president of gifting water bottles to thirsty
clients after their journey to 532 w. arbor vitae street,

where her office was like the [original] outdoor farmer's market
(before we had those in inglewood,)

except instead of papaya in vendors' hands, it was w-2s
and best bargain plastic bags filled with tangled receipts for accounting.

this small universe, the first real nation of all nations,
whose dominant language is a hug bridging

skins or unlocking the air of freedom trapped in a bomb
ass refund. some of her citizens brought the office plates of food, or asked

for me, *how is fabis*, her child prophet.
i sat in the corner of her office, star-eyed, noting

this was the north star people followed,
the map God placed before all peoples to find each other.

i stuffed my cruiser bike basket with stacks of pink,
yellow, and blue flyers i made on a free computer, boldly reading:

LORENZANA SERVICES, subtitled:
tax season!

over a picture of mami's office's front door and
stormed out. all of my people waved goodbye

as i, the president's daughter, took the streets
and waved flyers like a flag across the neighborhood

filling people's mailboxes and flashing
my big teeth at the passerbyers in my hood to *Come! Come to this nation,*

there's free hugs, and - and - come to this nation!
you can drink shots of joy and really rest, and my mom's

super nice! this nation, this warm customer service
is real, and it's on Arbor Vitae,

just down the street.

Learning English, a Than-Bauk

i am sometimes-girl/
i am curly-boy/
a whirl and mask/

a heavy task day/
don't ask/ i hide
my loud pride/ snakes

coil/ bribe/ flake skin
and shake kin/ fear/
i spin/ scrape bones/

i cower/ alone/ enjoy
the pelon's hard nub/
i'm definitely a girl/

she doesn't blush/ but
definitely hurls eye punches/
how many crushes did

i crunch softly tonight?/
i carry fright/ he
doesn't quite like me/

Coming Out or Undone

At fourteen I came out as bi in underwear next to my feet-swollen   mami. I came out as
gay at seventeen tired years old,   then came out as   undocumented

before high school   ended, then at twenty three, queer or   *cuír* as mami says it.
At 24 I held the steering wheel and I said,   *trans*, as mami listened to   the church in my

voice. *I forget the intended*
superficial function of thresholds: entry points or exits between one thing and

another, one space and
                    another.

My waist, wrapped in a leather dress, belongs to all things related to: the breeze, a lost fauna
covered trail in Japan, or the president's mahogany desk. My tangled, pink beard belongs every

where, like
          a white board in a classroom or the sweaty walls of a cis hetero club. My hoops belong
anywhere like an imported   rug on a millionaire's un-stepped-on-white   carpet.

          There is no bloody axe or plastic bags with dismembered limbs,   separate parts of me,
sprinkled across the desert. There is no denying the way I hook to all things living and   dead.

My body is not made of wood and straight edge   nails, mami, it is made of the desert's sandy
     lips,   tides of wind, everferescent scales on a chameleon's foot, or the veiny leaf

          pattern on a wild moth. Foreigners exist even in our family, with their marbling side-eyes
or strangers with angry placards shaming the creature in me,   shaming the way my
body slips from

          the flesh of
          mortals and into God.   The first time I saw Angel on Pose, God whispered in my

ear a declaration of   love. It was the first time I understood that thresholds are   man's
creation.   Does the sky ever end?

Where does the universe wrap itself   finished? Does it tie a knot at its tail and say:
Finito? Ya termine mi turno? At twenty-six years old I hear the private love whispers between

my hoops and beard, how they gossip about how much they're down to adopt   they
love my matte lip   trembling with Hot Cheetoh crumbs. *I knew that my*

        tears loved living so effortlessly
    during the Pose season premiere.

The universe created blades of grass   capable of protruding through the thickest of snow.
        Angel and I are

blades of grass not   *fiction.*
The beginning of time started with a towel wrapped around   my hair *I stood in*

front of the mirror singing como la flor as a kid do you remember? That's when I knew, ma,
I can stretch out in every direction and fool the eye into thinking I am   the sky.

Retrato in Names

Grandma calls me My Little Son with the way she digs her red acrylics into my plump hand, but utters Grandson, yet what she actually means to say is Daughter I Never Had Who I Love So Much because Mari, whom she calls My Little Daughter, was always more Tomboy. Patty, the Eldest Daughter, also known as Too Sickly, had a sensitive scalp. Grandma couldn't pull her hair for braids, so she used my hair to turn me into the girl I couldn't be. Curiosito, she would whisper in my ear, *weirdo*.

Grandpa calls me My King when he decides to speak to me, but what he actually means to call me is I Know You're a Princess and I Still Love You. I know this because he shares his grapefruit with me which is also called Amor Eterno according to my Grandma who I sometimes call Abuelita, Little Grandma. Grandpa who I sometimes call Abuelo is never called Little Grandpa because it makes him feel less like my father or less of a man.

Mami calls me My Little Dog and gives me a necklace with an expensive stone when I start dressing like a girl. Mami, who I sometimes call Mom, will text me throughout the day: My Son how are you today? On days she remembers she'll say My Life. Stray, Mami will sometimes call me, and bring me to her chest, hug me and fill the voids of men that leave me stranded. *You know that I love you so much right?*, she says with tears in her eyes and goes back to clicking plastic keys on a keyboard, and someone will shout her name, Boss You Have a Client Question.

Madrina calls me My Boy because she lost her firstborn and I replaced him. I sometimes call her My Second Mom or Tia Patty or Mean because she's all those things, but never to her face. Tia is the name I use when I knock on her rusted door from her soon-to-be-foreclosed house. Life Did You So Wrong I Empathize With You always pops more pills than she should because the pain is insurmountable or the high is too good. Even though she calls me My Sky or My Treasure, I still can only sometimes call her I Know You're Hurting But That's Not An Excuse To Hurt Others.

Padrino, who I can only ever call Tio Martin, or Dad I Never Had in birthday cards, calls me Fabis, a name that yanked free of my hand. He remembers calling me My Little Boy a year ago, but now that I dress like a girl he says Silence. Sometimes I know he wants to call me This Lifestyle Isn't Right, but he won't, instead he'll call me by my name, Strange or I Don't Understand You. Regardless, I'll be the first he whips a plate of carne asada even though I don't eat meat, beans, avocado, and nopal salad for when I walk into his house in rapture. He's the only person I have ever called Father even when I don't show up to his midnight birthday cake candle-blow-out.

Suseth, I sometimes call Susie, or Sue, or Angry Ass Bitch because she's stank ever since college, even though when we were younger I called her Me. She calls me Annoying or Brother or Sister but mostly she doesn't call me. I mostly call her Sister, but in a tone you use when you want to say more but don't, the way you put glass cups in a cardboard box for storage. Sometimes she'll surprise me with kindness and transparency and I'll call her Open Heart Surgery Survivor or Your Softness Inspires Me or Thank You For the Tortillas You Just Handmade for Me or Your Salsa is the Best But Damn Were You Mad? Although we forget our first names to each other, our last name is Halcyon or Les Kick Et and that will never change.

Susie is also the first to correct our family when they don't use my correct pronouns. *They, Them, Their, is the pronouns My Sister needs us to use for them!*

I never call Natalia by her first name. That name is reserved for Mean when she slaps words at her daughter. To me, Natalia is Naty or My Baby, or Dayuum You Cooked This Bomb Ass Cake? or Nana or Nani. Nani is also Holder Of Everyone's Pain But I Won't Cry or The Baddest Bitch I Know. Although Tia Patty thinks Open Heart Surgery Survivor and My Baby her hands, Nana is Stank Face Cus I'm Not Gonna Say Shit when she's fed up. Naty is sometimes I'm Tired Of All Y'alls Shit I'm Never Coming Back, but sometimes she's First To Shed Tears When The Family Hurt. Nana calls me Billy, a nickname I took on in high school to be anything but Undocumented, Faggot, Mad. She calls me DAMN YOU FINE or Dummmmmm, or Your Hoops Are Poppin Bitch, but she usually addresses me as Home Away From House or Safe Space or Thank You For Holding Me, For Taking Care of Me. Nana, my Frizzy Haired Wild Woman teaches me the intricacies of love over a quiet phone call.

Corazón

It is 5:45am yet you say you choose my smile over the sun/ *Dormilon*/
You take the sunlight like my body and say you'd rather hold me than dream/

We're going to have a great day/ you say with a *tierna sonrisa*/
But I can't help but think that these are borrowed words/ I bet *asi le dices a todos*/

You turn and pull a strand of rose quartz from your counter drawer/ a return item so today
will have a tomorrow/ and latch it around my naked neck/ *Quedatelo*/ But I don't believe you/

I eye roll/ but there is nowhere to hide my wild *carcajada* that rises up from a hidden corner inside me/
My face drops its guard and a smile blooms like *girasoles* across my face with your *chistes*/

How do your almond eyes focus on me like photo lenses and capture me
in ways hands never have before?/ *Me gustas* / you say without words/

But enters *incertidumbre*/ enters my exes/ and feelings of unworthiness/

Boyyyyy/ I keep scrolling through reasons why you should choose
the sun over me/ your ex over me/ the next best guy over me/

I go from wanting to be the dirt under a vaseless lily/ unseen and unwatered/
to being *al menos*/ *la luna llena* you stare at when you daydream in broad daylight/

Sometimes/ I'd rather be the water rings on your coffee table/ than *tu media naranja*
that can go bad if cut and not eaten/

You ask me to stay the night/ but what does it mean to stay forever?/
I am not used to a man asking me reassuringly to join them in anything close to freedom/

You keep my toothbrush next to yours/ My towel next to yours/ You say your bed's cold
without me/ In a mocking tone you reply to my insecurities/ Boyyyyy / the sun beaming perfectly

on your face/ *stay the night*/ *Quédate*/ There is no escaping your naked eye as we intertwine
our tender bodies as one/ You call me by my name/

Muse / For once I lose the fear and unlock my hips/ ground myself
in being open/ in being your sunrise even at night/

(un)Documented: *Answers I (Didn't) Give USCIS*

Being undocumented is a state inside the mind,
      the only territory we have receipts of that prove we lived   there or anywhere.

After being questioned by my legal "father" to be, who's obviously not my biological father,
      but the "father" only interested in charging us more oxygen than we can

fit in a water gallon, I became silent. He was mouth, it seemed, since I lost every word I
      ever learned and replaced it with dry throat before the American state.

Even after the white USCIS man's blue eyes that remind me of camera lenses or West
      Hollywood gays, traced my geography, in other words my ass, I fake-smiled.

I could be swallowable, I thought, so maybe, just maybe, he'll let the citizen in me run free?
      Even with my green card in its worn down slip two years later, even

after the quiet ceremony of my new citizenship status, the sad couches in my living
      room sighed. I had the bright idea to ask mami a rhetorical question,

Are we actually safe?

Years later I had a polished American passport in my back pocket and another brilliant question
      broke free from my child-adult mouth as she drove us to Best Bargain for groceries,

Are we actually safe?

To which she replied, *we've only ever answered to the desert's call inside our mind,*
      the only geography we have receipts of that prove we lived there.

So yes, Little Dog, we belong to ourselves and wherever we go as long as we're together. And
no   *we're not safe. Yet, I would still love to be an American Citizen.*

Ángel de la Guardia

mighty tall like a palm tree / he looks down / at the ant of me / fisheye / lens / follows me / traces my drunk cruiser bike zigzagging / round the new speed bumps /

my savior / my God / stands above me with feet in cement / my only ángel de la guardia / brown body with black fingers / holding every piece of heaven / his fingers adorned with black silver birds /

his fingers / nets / in case I fall into Inglewood from the sky / again /
a lost star / on display while a spaceship / peruses in front of Randy's on wheels / my God /

always holds something / the memory of an alley fight / a mouse in the grip of a silver-black bird / drive-bys / a homie smacking / his baby momma / there is no corner my angel don't / post up at /

chin up / casts a skinny shadow / over the back-homes we lived in / over the empty lots with fickle weeds / peeking their head through netted fences /

out of hiding / out the closet / my God / hides me / my obese / tired body / with its skinny shadow / while I gasp for breath / looking / side-to-side / on the hottest day in Inglewood / my angel

spreads its wings for me / while I repair / the loose chain of me on a corner / my hands bloodied with grease / the bare toothed sidewalks laugh at me / the alley fights roar / I hope Eddy is okay /

Momo didn't get shot? / thank

God / I'll call you later / and when the heat recedes and the ocean mist flocks the bruised streets / my angel / vibrates with the heat of phone calls / shooting through its arms /

mothers call their children /

my God holds witness that she called / even though she knew que / Dios me cuida / ba / telepathized my angel that followed me / block to block / knowing / he watched the ant / of me / memorizing the streets /

potholes / the last places people were seen / alive / pointing at all my friend's homes / lit in the evening glow / eating dinner as a family / I memorized the streets to make sure I knew where I came from /

my angel / my mom / taught me how to love / my sky / sliced /
and be grateful / for our slice / be full / with the piece of life we have /

Citing Sources

Fingerprints in blood, who cares about ink.
There is no mirror that can pull your grandmother from your nose.

How do you cite where the bark was sliced and where the men in tire-rubber sandals dropped
from cliffs? Did their mouths become the rocks breaking the crash? Is the only way to reach

ancestors to jump? When your mother tucks cuentos into your trenzas she hopes you'll write them.
Stop avoiding the mucus-covered beans on your plate. They is history.

Before the jury, hold a needleless cactus into the air and promise you they'll understand.
Let's look at this from a different angle. Break the skin.

Under that land of muscles is a plethora of purple rivers tied to places in the sky.
If you don't believe in the moon and sun cycling under your antepasados, who will?

Brunch

Look/ America is Black/ therefore Indigenous/ home to native peoples in the Americas/ PERIODT/ I grew up in Inglewood/ I am a non-Black person of color/ was taught African American vernacular until all the conditionings/ all types of code switching/ ways of talking/ in Mexican/ even in code/ in grafitti/ or silence meshed together/ all the types of English/ Inglewood English/ Immigrant English/ pass me the hot sauce/ Hand Gesturing English/ NYC slang from when I lived there for a minute/ I know you said the drinks were bomb here, but look at all these white people/ an English full in its brokeness inside me/ yet I'm still broke/ brooooooke/ I'm HELLA light skint, bruh/ but before I am undocumented/ or queer as fuck/ I maneuver the world through race first/ or rather/ skin color/ I know you're spotting me, but are you sure? It's hella expensive b!/ colorism still defines the wold/ this anti-Black and indigenous world we live in/ yo this shit needs salt, pass it to me/ I am not looked at in the same ways that my Black kin are/ light skint/ white-passing ass/ poc/ need to check their privileges/ and that's not to deny my transness/ or all the other intersections of identity/ I know/ yes my lip be poppin' and is a bold ass color every time, but/ damn, this drink is so good, bitch!/ so yes, people be lookin' at me/ homophobes/ be pestering and side-eyeing me/ pulling me from me/ and yes transphobic ass motherfuckers/ wanna look/ leave that mal de ojo that stays leaves me dissociated/ body dysmorphic/ gender dysphoric/ and shit/ but/ do cops size me up/ look at me/ the same way they do my Black trans sisters?/ am I systematically surveyed and disenfranchised or disrespected the way my dark skint kin are?/ no/ This is how I look out/ for my community/ the all inclusive/ not just hegemonic/ mexican/ undocumeted/ centric/ "community"/ I mean real-real community/ where the people I fuck with are operating from honest/ true/ intersectionality/ these pancakes are aight, but we coulda had better ones at Astro's/ side-eye/ also, look at how these white ass waiters look at us everytime I ask for more ranch/ mega eyeroll/ e-ny-ways, b, I am here to support the cackle of my homies, and our growth/ in safety/ burning cop cars/ bridging and upholding our differences/ showing up like fr fr/ aiding each other/ like I'm talking bout resources, real resources/ checking in-in/ through heart/ moving in unison/ like really being there/ not resting until shit changes/ hold up tho, let me take a bite/ Yo, I remember a three way call with Ebony/ Portia/ Justin/ how inseperable we were/ until we were/ how we played with our hair while we talked about mad shit/ you think she's a lesbian?/ we were talking about some girl in our class/ but we are all curious/ cus we all had a lil something/ queer about us/ we were fools doe/ learned so much about life through our differences/ at a young age/ I couldn't help, but see the world/ like really see it/ like/ check my own privileges amidst my own hardships/ I learned how to reach the human in me/ while being aware of the systematic/ people out here stay operating from what little they actually know/ those pseudo woke hos be blowin' mine/ telling me I'm extra/ or to let it go/ my identities can't exist without the context of Blackness/ I can not learn myself without understanding/ I'm sorry, I won't pound the table again/ and loving Blackness/ yes, my Abuelita's grandma was/ Pi'ma/ and my dad's grandmother was/ Tarahumara/ but I don't go around saying I'm native either/ FOH/ that blue drink looks so fucken good! Is it an Adios?/ everyone has their place in the revolution/ my place is in the liminal/ intersectional spaces of belonging/ bridging and dismantaling/ the only reason why I'm who I am is because Black folks made me/ rich gold melanin is what keeps all of us thriving and going/ it's what dismantles the systems that oppress us by simply existing/ keeps us evolving/ shedding light to the brokeness that is America/ the world/ I said I wouldn't shake the table, my bad/ I know, I know, everyone's looking/ white people and poc just don't be getting it/ their responsibility/ to making shit change for the betterment of Black folk/ like real change/ and hold their own accountable/ I know I'm preaching, but anti-Blackness is NOT new/ white people and poc need to get it togetha/ need to have been showing up for Black trans femmes non-binary and intersex folks yesterday!/ but anyways/ buy me a shot b/ these fools and their activisty posts are blowin mine/ you shoudn't have showed me homeboy's IG post/ pass me the syrup, my pancakes are dumb dry/ where were folks twenty years, thirty fifty years ago, huh? / what about a hundred years ago? like/ look at all these people/ eating and shit without a/ worry! Like/

Flower Lasso

apa is skilled in the rodeo.
He surfs the saddle of his black
stallion and brings the halo
he lassos around the sun

down to the hellish cloud
of dirt and hoove-printed
dance floor. The roaring crowd
whistles and thunder-claps apa's

Flower Lasso, the ultimate
floreo in colonized history.
apa's crimson wrist
orbits with the strength of sand

storms and Tarahumara grandmothers.
apa lifts his stallion on hind legs,
meets the saddle, and summons
his father in the sky above him.

     Floreo.

The cages are opened by stampede.
apa's dust trail kicks when calf
bulls scurry across the rodeo.
He swings fast lassos around bulging

bull necks and running hooves. Apa
sweats and breaks his body down in northern
traditions to conjure the memory of his father.
His flared face is a gap tooth smile.

This is how he wakes my grandfather
from ashes on lonely days. This is how he wraps
his father in a noose so he can learn how to be
a father to the child he aborted to the wind.

This is how he repents. This is how he hands me heirlooms,
answers for how to catch him alive,
how to restore his memory in good-light:
      dust, open sky, Flower Lasso, applause.

𝔚𝔥𝔦𝔱𝔢 𝔐𝔞𝔫

slurps iced coffee and diagnoses me with PTSD.
After avoiding: deportation, a shooter drill scare, and heartbreak I smirk.
My attention is on the Desert Rose mineral on the other side of the room, not his blue eyes.

~~White Man~~ marks my story in red as I talk. Each mark a slap across the table, a "new" diagnosis.
After avoiding: deportation, a shooter drill scare, and heartbreak I sigh.
No…I think the PTSD is not from recent events, it's my mother's. Cellular memory. Ya know?

~~White Man~~ marks my story in red as I talk, each mark a slap across the table, a new diagnosis.
~~White Man~~ scoffs, No, Your diagnosis is strictly from current events.
Nah. I know the PTSD is not from recent events, Doctor. I found it in my mother.

The devil is my twin brother no one found. He's who roars in my head when I can't sleep.
~~White Man~~ scoffs, *No, Your diagnosis is strictly from current events.*
Mami, pregnant with me, fled México to avoid being target practice for my father's wife.

The devil is my twin brother no one found. He's who roars in my head when I can't sleep.
Mami leaves my father in the desert alone and escapes to a new country that hates us.
Mami, pregnant with me, left her home to ensure we didn't die at the hands of an angry wife.

~~White Man~~ "confirms" my PTSD was triggered in the classroom during the shooter drill. *Okay?*
Gunshots pierced the air from angry-wife's rifle, colossal rock crunched mami's car.
I avert my attention to the Desert Rose mineral sitting on the other side of the room and eyeroll.

~~White Man~~ confirms my PTSD was triggered in the classroom during the shooter drill. *Okay?*
You can't blame the devil—your brother is not real after all, he says.
~~White Man~~ slurps iced coffee and wrongly diagnoses the cause of my PTSD.

The Hood Criatura

thick thighs made out of bull catapult forward   wrapped in dark denim the   sky swallows the bark or howl or deep throat roar of a wild beast on hind legs fangs out and crushed

ojos the color of mandarina   tiny wheels on blue asphalt brrrrrrrr   ghosts of dust follow and red sneakers   thrust harder while the sidewalk moans   and he still can't reach his

shadow   the plastic board pushes forward into quiet darkness   except for sirens and cop cars   and occasional hood birds chirping in bushes   there is

no sound or cabra bleeding to death   no possessed savage beast behind a farm   just the smell of spray paint weed sweat   sweaters   wet grass   no   he's not a hysterical howling

woman   white veil over her face   this creature never had children but the ones drizzled in his mouth   after men leave   criatura is another word for beast or

child   he is not hunched with protruding claws no slithering tongue slipping past fat wet lips or body hair that makes hunters think it   slayable   but it's like a doll's

        this criatura is kawaii   like gloomy bear   wears bright colors like yellow upstream salmon pink   anime baby blue cap   his gums show their leg during cackle

        the glimmer of its glasses under the street light on Arbor Vitae   spotlight on a nerd who follows his boy crush   trails him like prey all   red-eyed thirsty and shit down an

avenue named after   the Tree of Life   what a coincidence that all things ugly tossed into folklore out of fear   scratch their way out of myth

how this criatura found the hood lake where all   Black and Brown souls return to   who knows?   it can be found at a nearby river writing words like *mercurial*

in sketchbooks over   weed sprawled pools under the horned moon laughing dreaming about boys in the nearby apartments   so much disdain is dumped on its body always

        mistaken for danger   the beast holds a scribbled poem to the light   what an unseemly sacrifice a beast offers to the night   a ferocious lyricist the giggling monster is

Inglewood's Eddy

Eddy skates faster than me. Skinny, hairy legs kick him forward, surfs Inglewood concrete like the Silver Rider. Except he's not silver but brown, scar on his left eyebrow, scrawny with shorts and a white T too big for him. He currently has a purple half moon on his right cheek—failed alley fight. It hurts him to smile at me, but he still does.

It's a couple blocks before we make it to the weed-fogged Ash Park near the 405. Eddy is my first friend. He licks his lips before he speaks. Has a fresh line up and cracks his knuckles. Arms are dipped in ink skulls, Iztaccihuatl, and his mom's name. Cackles like a drunk lizard on a mariachi's shoulder. I want to be the smoke he blows out from deep inside him. *But he can never know this.* His homies are right across the netted fence near the tagged picnic tables in basketball shorts, laughing, legs wide open. I don't look in between. Instead I study the wrinkles on the paper bags they drink from. Joints on their fingertips. Their custom tatts. I look right through them for fear of finding something more.

They all eye me, the clumsy, sidewalk-crack stumbling Fat Boy with shirts too-dark, too-tight around his lonjas, his hair always covering his eyes. They eye Eddy like: *why you hanging out with that faggot.* Eddy leans in for the hand-smack-hug, reassuring them of his allegiance to them and wraps an arm around me to claim me. He shatters their masculinity, pulls smiles from them by being jokester, gentle, drug dealer, homie, friend. I make his homies re-adjust their jaw and sit up right. Homies look down at me from the sky as I get closer. The stench of cologne and sweat off their skin, territory mark. This turns me on instead of cower, but I look down to give them their moment. Men need reassurances too. I nod, greet them from afar. Eddy digs his hand in his shirt while he speaks. I follow the trail of hair under his belly button and chiseled abs, his skin the color of the sun and coffee—I want to be his sky.

"That homie RAN! I punched him hard, then he swung and half hit my face, then he ran down the fucken alley, dude!"

His homies nod thru the story, have trouble speaking, eyes too red. In the corner of the group a chubby, colossal man named Tiro, in a wife-beater takes a hit of his joint.

"But imma get that foo back, FO SHO! Let me catch him slippin'."

The joint makes its way to me, but I pass it directly to Eddy. He takes a hit. All I do is pretend his lips kiss mine. His full lips. Wet. Through the cloud of smoke around his smile I avert my glance. But hold that moment in my stomach, a picture I'll return to later at night. Tiro chuckles with slanted red eyes and looks at me, says "I know your secret," but I don't think he actually says this, I'm probably just contact high, so I walk away with my sketchbook.

The sun sets after a game or two of basketball. Sweaty, tattooed brown men in basketball shorts run back and forth like in my dreams. Eddy comes around, sweat dripping from his face, winks at me and darts back to the game. I think of my name in graffiti letters. The drawing he made for me in Mr. Ford's class. We leave the park in silence. The palm trees sway and mock the sound of the ocean. He pushes himself forward on his skateboard. I know he's gonna tag on our way home. Hopefully it's my name. He's the Silver Rider—except he's not silver but brown, scar on his left eyebrow, scrawny with shorts and a white T too big for him. He's no hero saving the city from crime. He is the love of my life. He is the love of my life. He is the love of my life.

The palm trees sway harder and the waves of their sound roar. Eddy. No matter how fast I am, my stubby legs will not reach him. He is always a little too far out of my touch. But he looks back and waves for me to hurry up the way he does,

"FAT BOY. LET'S GO! Hurry up!"

"Please Sing Along"

My students, flower Black and Brown bodies
tucked in coffin uniforms, stand for the pledge of allegiance.

They hold the flag with their gaze, the flag a circling eagle.
Their tiny hand over their heart. They invest roots in the American project

blindly, yet dig their toes past dead earth searching for a different kind of food
they don't even know they crave yet.

During the morning assembly, I point at the eagle with my index finger,
click the crank with my thumb to break the illusion.

Sometimes I am not Teacher but the little boy made of hard clay
who doesn't speak English in fear of cracking, the one

who wasn't taught that death language. Sometimes as I stand as a teacher, I am
taken back to the hypnosis of my elementary school assembly

where the devil in a white suit introduced himself to me.
His name was: Yellow Teeth. Gold Hair Shaking Like Slow Lightning.

His name was: Pale Hand or Principal. I can't remember. But he nudged me,
Wave the flag in your mouth—he said, *Sing along.*

*

On my first day of teaching, I pledge under my breath,
introduce myself as fiction pulled out of the bounds of a novel.

Tell them my story and compare myself to an empty brown paper bag,
the worst kind of paper to cut for decorative

Mexican papel picado. When they hang me for display,
I don't even sway. I am stiff cardboard against breeze. I was already dead

before the puncturing.
Two weeks into teaching:

I am a frozen teacher behind a long desk.
My student's eyes hold a ruler to me—

Why don't you say the pledge of allegiance?
Where is the flag in your mouth?

Don't you love America? Why do you hate white people?
3 months into teaching:

I call out the anti-Blackness in the classroom. I remind them our Black
kin are target practice, their bodies, entry ways for bullets.

The Protest Placard Unit, the Refugee Unit, the Identity Unit all held
a mirror to each student and reminded them the U.S. has hit its target:

our shape-shifting spine, our undying tongues, our mystic eyes,
our pulsing veins. 5 trans identified students came out to me during lunch that week.

I remind my students in silence that shackles are loud with death statistics.
My students make banners to welcome Central American immigrants despised

by the U.S. and Mexico. I remind them Black trans
women are deemed disposable in the U.S.A., their bodies uncounted.

We pledge to stop all cops,
We pledge to have each other's back.

We pledge to turn white supremacy to dust,
We pledge to write our stories, amen.

35 weeks into teaching I almost get deported. The next day during the morning
assembly I slip out of teacher and become the little boy made of hard clay.

Instead of announcements and class chants, I hear the scrubbing of a pumix rock
against callus in a distant corner. My students before me turn into seeds

and wiggle into the earth and the blackboard, the agenda, runs out of the classroom.
London Haynes follows me as I pace around the classroom and asks me,

is the clay boy inside you okay?
Atziri Sanchez tells me, *it's okay to sit quietly Mx. Shumari.*

It's okay if you don't know the words to the pledge.
Kay Dixon hands me community guidelines we wrote together two weeks

into school and forces me to read it out loud to the class.
I pledge allegiance to the fight,

I pledge to the Indigenous and Black abuelas, abuelos,
to our great grandparents that died in protest for us,

that picked cotton and jumped walls for us.
I pledge allegiance to horchata and fried chicken,

to the liminal space of identity.
To love that is beyond our differences.

I pledge allegiance to the fight against
Capitalism. I pledge to defend Inglewood from gentrification.

I pledge against a world seeking to silence us,
I pledge allegiance to a new world.

A new world. A new world,
a new world.

Apa Nagual

It is the habit for Little Grandpa to blend in with the trees.
He disguises himself bark hands full of flowers and fruit.
There is no better companion for him than seeds or Open Sky.

He is of the kind of nature that clenches the Earth when he's beneath it and chews.

Little Grandpa's leaves rustle and you can hear the pecking of his
fingers on an orange or pomegranate checking its pulse. Pickaxe slicing wood in the distance.
The tightness of the fruit cracked open releases smells of a time when Little

Grandpa's feet kicked coffee beans into air to feed the sky,

kicked memories across a field of tall swaying grass. His little boy body like his old boy
body is the color of mud. Blue. All things that fall off branches are desperate to be swallowed by his two
hands including my heart and be smothered into his flesh, his grumbling intestines.

No one questions my Little Grandpa and the way he sits alone under a grapefruit tree.

No one questions the magic he lends himself to. When his smile spreads
the desert shifts until it is comfortable in its purple setting.
I've asked him how he feels about what my family has to say about his "way of being":

slow, inconsiderate, passively demanding.

Little Grandpa says _____.
I've asked him what he wants to do with the rest of his days to which
he replies _____.

An orange coil falls to the floor and he lifts a skinless pulping heart into the air.
He digs his finger into my crevice without remorse. Little Grandpa holds one half of orange in each
hand and places the bloodiest one in my little boy palm.

You get half the orange for sharing this day with me, he says in a child's voice.

Lala the Origin
or Futuristic Magical Realist Text Sample

Anyone who enters illegally what is now
the United States knows to meet with Lala

before the chip is implanted in the left
arm where the blue veins converge.

She no longer needs a red headband to
cover her eyes, she sees through a single yellow

eye on her forehead, even under all her wild
green hair. Lala's cavern smells like seaweed—walls,

wet scales, the floor, mud. There is a giant oak her home
shades under, invisible to legals.

Lala will hand you a mucus-covered cactus
needle as soon as you enter and you will not speak.

She will rub your stomach three times
clockwise after lying down. The payment is your other half:

sometimes ancient coins, sometimes black and white
photographs of you in another country, now on fire.

Sometimes whole lovers are sacrificed—their blood for the sake
of awakening your shapeshifting gene, but it all depends on your karmic debt.

Her brown, bluing hands are wide and fast—a bird's beak
claiming food mid-air. The mucus-covered cactus

needle must be quickly swallowed while the tense
gut is rearranged and molded to vaccinate mental enslavement.

There are long lines of people who curve around
hood apartments of those who just crossed

outside of Lala's cavern. Seasons will pass,
but all aliens know better than to lose their place in line—

Lala is the only way to survive this country of closed doors,
trackers, and syringes. She is a coyote, a witch, a mother from the sea.

Lala will place her hands on your pelvis after animalistically
devouring a bundle of your hair. In tongues she will say,

Black wings will grow from your hips after the cactus
needle mixes with bile. Let your blue organs free you.

Her single yellow eye will
follow your every move.

She will spit into the smoke and slice
a guayaba in half and without thought you will drop

to your knees, sink deep into the mud, and remember your native
country before the fire, before your DNA helix was torn.

When you wake up three days later cocooned in mud, she will hand you
two tequila shots and will ask you to take your clothes off.

She will dig her hands in a wooden bowl the size of a torso—
pull out from its depth two handfuls of honey and rub

them across your bare chest. She will say, *The beings from the moon*
before us did this ritual to become the ignorant we are now.

Give your body back. We need to be mighty
blue, tongueless gods again.

In three days your skin will begin to blue. In time
your eyes will yellow, your movements will be fast,

more precise. You will age slower and you will not be able to avoid swimming
the depths of the nearest green body of water on days of freedom.

When They Leave, a Pantoum

They will take my Ma, Little Girl, when they leave.
Little Girl runs into the dark cobblestone hallway mid night.
Ma is a devoted, pious Little Daughter.
I lost Mom in the new country.

Little Girl runs into the dark end of a long street mid night.
When my Little Grandparents die she will snuggle in their casket.
I lost Mom in the new country.
My Little Grandparents raised me when Little Girl wasn't around.

When My Little Grandparents die Mami will chew on their bones.
Little Girl gets out of her car in the middle of traffic, teetering teeth, hungry.
My Little Grandparents raised me when Mom worked night shifts.
Little Girl walks back home from work to check My Little Grandparent's pulse.

Malooksthrou
ghtheirwindo
wtoseeiftheyar
ealive.

Mom sprints out of the car in the middle of traffic to get home before they die.
Little Girl is my Mami in a new country, yet her memory begins to skip my birth date.
Mami is desperate to see my Little Grandparents after work, but not me, her Little Dog.
Mom forgets she has a Little Dog at school during a 90s earthquake, but I'm okay.

Mami is in a new country, but only cares to be a Perfect Daughter or Little Girl.
Ma is a devoted, pious Little Daughter
willing to forget her Little Dog to eternally be Little Girl again and not my Ma, Ma, Ma.
My Little Grandparents will drag my Mami deeper into their rattling grave when they turn.

City of Champions

black and brown children still
born or born laughin play in jungle

gyms black and brown moms
push carts filled with ebt shnaks while

talkin with their girls out loud
hand gesturin play arguin or actually

fightin be it flip phone blackberry iphone
some daddys in button up

shirts set up bbq at the pit of the city centinela
park some daddys can only play

on sundays usin caller cards across the border
some daddys are uncles who lather

their mommies' round nose wait for the red
lipstick kiss print on their skin

la brea's organs pump keep the blood flowin
ligaments reverberate after smack

a cord or a chancla hyde park trebles with loud
hip hop or gangster shit through

tinted windows hydraulics or bikes lifted on one
wheel while the weed hit good

mariachis play the heart throbs and wangs even
when arbor vitae's neck is gripped

we smile our brave teeth even when choked
harder by a villain trying to

suffocate black dreams brown dreams black and
brown children dreams who

raw cow with beer at rogers park or tony
siminski park where mad kids have

their first birthday party balloons forget to grip
the metal bar they were tied to

at birth and fly out of inglewood's hot mouth
brown and black babies in

miniature jordans or vans don't cry reach for the
moon in broad daylight giggle at

seedlings grew tall thigh-strong we thrive we
manifest in the dark

a champion is a call to action to be
even when we don't want to cus shit's

hard even when your bed is tossed past
the stratosphere over night because

were brought here or watered and planted in the
wound of this city before the rib

cage of a metal stadium was stripped of flesh and
opened before us hollywood

park casino was kicked into dust before potholes
were covered and the seeds

burrowed in those concrete holes defied
the anatomy of what makes a garden

never did we tell our parents we love them in
silence cus they be dumb extra

sometimes with their catholic guilt or their
gamblin or their silence or smacks

pinches or the way we gotta parent them
sometimes we say we love ya'll

beyond the cheatin the drivebys the let downs
the sound of laughter

heavy ass convos followed yet when the gigglin
ends and the air stops we hear

metal clankin a drill on crenshaw and orange
cones digress our sharp right then

legislation or lack of rent control or a city
meeting people can't attend cus its

during work hours to be a champion is to be all
your broken pieces know you the

only you so crack jokes with your homies about
anythin do voice overs on

couples arguin or our mommas and their novelas
the next morning none of us

expect a school bus yellow tractor to lift the
streets we drove manchester century

all cracked like bad acne and with it our patience
cus traffic exists where it

left turn into our apartments i mean
homes cus we don't believe we can live

in a big ass house like they do down the
street all the way down the street

edge of the world or playa del rey so we
call anything we can home but we

got our black owned coffee shops and
galleries and we have the brown

mamas and their thrivin tax or hair
salons or the homies new barber shop or

star donut that i like way more than randy's cus
you know they sell that hand

scoop ice cream in foam cups but whatever the
point is we won't stop even if

the baby shower balloons get tangled
on telephone wires or make their way out

of the mouth of kelso street dead or alive
or the cops show up with some bullshit

we moan with the metal skeleton that
doesn't know its name and even when

we've tried to undo our memory it's beyond
us to be anything greater than this

here resilience amidst the deep purple pain
that floods the veins of la cienega

the city is sick unrooted apartments pulse
blue with internal bruisin yet the organs

bump to a track we call joy we call this
inglewood our home and we rep

Pop-Lock-and-Drop-It

On the east coast
while white families across the street
put up confederate flags on their homes
Black and Brown students

bump-and-grinded in sweaty
apartments. I used to shake my ass
on the dance floor and my people'd be like:
OH, OH-KAY! I see you Inglewood, C'mon!

Now, the only elbow nudge is my violent voice
filled with cop sirens policing me to *shrink*.
What happened to my hip and sway during bachata? Did my stanky
leg and cat daddy slip along with my place to belong?

Did college chew my pop-lock-and-drop-it when it enforced the
disease that split a nation and how undeserving I am to love myself,

therefore my people?

My People

*[This morning Fatimah Asghar
asks, "How many people can I make my people?"
in VS Podcast hosted by Danez Smith and Franny Choi,
the MFA program I can afford or heaven.]*

I am left puzzled
when I can't paint a portrait of my country
or the bamboo hooped earrings the curvy
women that made me wear. There is no

dissertation long enough to detail the array of sazón in all of our foods. We all different.
How do I delineate the ways big lips that drop heavy words and smack bubble
gum made me? How can I fit all my people into a teeny abstract in summary of what is
my people. My people are made of curly and straight hair and skin the color of abyss and maiz.

They are made of light that welcome foreign bodies into family and there's no equation to it.
There are no theories that can take you to the dispossessed, the stranded ones in the in-between
threshold, the half-born, or kaleidoscopic dream place we doze off to unless you are my people.
Tonight I think about how empty handed feeling full is. You carry your people in your traveling

womb not your fingers liking everybody just to like em. How filling it is to love with your gut
and your fists. For example, two days ago my silhouette rode a bus as a sad-orange sunset
slurped itself into a Mexican purple mountain range. I had a pending convo with one of my
people. Dad's truck coughed and caved in on the lightless shoulder of a highway. We counted

the stars like the years we'd missed and the words we didn't say that night. There's no way to
explain how many people are my people aside from: I forgive you, father.
Is that a good sentence starter for a life committed to being an accomplice to all my people?
Today, I'm traveling the dusty cobblestone streets of El Centro, Chihuahua City's ancient heart,

and I see a Tarahumara woman in her neon-bright dress walk by me, but she didn't recognize me as a lost
child that also belongs to other people, probably also her people! Aside from being born from this gust of
wind I'm fighting against this Mexican-December and I can't help but miss my Inglewood. My people are
my destination, to and from. Across country lines, in Philly, in Japan. There's no way to quantify how
pregnant I

can be housing all the people I will always love, always love, even if we don't talk no more.

What Remains of Dad, a Portrait

drives white   painted bus to

sombrero   and

vaquero
norteño   from
gap-toothed
smile

sombrero
norteño   maquiladora
gallina   WhatsApp
maquiladoras   gap

cOmo esta mijo   horse-

leather skin   stomped

gallina   hand

gap-   holamijo
toothed   como
smile   hen

horse   norteño   esta

stomped
como
esta
mijo
gap-toothed smile

horse-stomped hand   maquiladoras

WhatsApp sombrero   from
norteño   and

hola mijo como esta
gallina   buses to
hen
gap-   paint
toothed smile   white
norteño   gap-toothed smile horse-stomped hand   drive

The Kind of Woman

Frida sits leg crossed with a cigarette in hand
marveling the scars on my sleeve

Did you stitch the flowers yourself?
Frida knows I too hide my broken body under long folklorico dresses

knows I tuck my scoliosis into my underwear knows my irregular
step the one that got me walking like a burro

knows my breast haven't grown wings
knows they're not free

She says   *It's okay to be crooked sometimes*
it's okay not to have floorboards to stand on in the body you were born in

Frida follows the embroidered blue flowers along my chest   *Dead river veins*
knows I stitched them with the hand of a clumsy Tarahumara child in learning

compliments the lost mestizo in me the exquisite mixed terrain of Mexican and passion
I've made out of suffering

stitchings on my clothes in every color even heartbreak again
and again   Frida passes me a bowl of cold fossilized fruit   *Even the dead eat she says*

so eat   She confesses my hoop earrings are good omens   like her
says *Your jewelry is the perfect temple to house the divine feminine in you*

          the devil la llorona and all the unresolved myths in you then   fixes the slanted jalapeño
plant sticking out from my trenzas   replants my desiccated thoughts   readjusts the stem upright

to heaven   uses my cascading tears to water me back to life and says   *here is a*
paintbrush   *pinta*

She drunkenly holds a portrait of Diego and herself against my child face   looks for me in them
almost makes an ashtray out of me the way she fingers her cigarette   but knows

I'm made of too much glass to burn   so she doesn't worry I'll catch fire like her wooden leg then stops   Frida caresses the daughter in me she couldn't womb   asks the

unasked   *Do you tuck your wings between your thighs too? Do you dream of standing without feet?*
Is your skeleton neither female

nor male?   Can you come with me where I am forever?
You are just like your father   she says   *You handle your menstruation the way*

Diego did on full moons   Frida laughs into a sob at the magic of this moment
only a table between us   years apart sewn together   she laughs and paints the air

with her finger the way we do in another life where we all stand together   naked under moon-silk
veils   *My baby*   she sings me a song   *I've missed you*

        Frida confesses Diego was a woman in mourning too
        Frida confesses she was a man too

Frida lifts my arms outstretched   guides me in feather stretches
she knows more about being a bird than me   exclaims I'm too tense for flight

reminds me of the ancient woman I am   *Culebra*   *or was it the holy virgin?*
Hmmmmm   *doesn't matter*   *they both fly*

Frida is now late for the day of the dead   Día De Los Muertos   an art show curated by drunken
observers   and haloless angels

God or Diego whisper in her ear   ask her to come back   the wind lifts her from her seat   joins
the sky without a cane mid-way dead   mid-way mother in flesh   she touches my glass

leg   enchants it to grow skin and toes   *In time you will run*   she leaves a note in my palms
instructions   teaches me the anatomy of spines the way they can realign no matter how

many nails unhook and fall
no matter how many hinges   unhinge and how many vertebrae slide   off

tells me again that crooked looks good on me   *It runs in the family*
then leaves me with a loud echoed whisper that wakes me:

You are the type of woman I love
for you I'll be late to any art show or heaven especially the one called   eternity

now baby   live
be free   be the woman you are as you are

Wounded Deer

If it weren't for the deer flesh that makes me
I'd be untangled stars laid on blue asphalt.
What is consent to the weight of living but a ghost?
Whose body do I dance with when I'm drunk?

I'd be untangled hair laid on blue asphalt
if only I'd been given permission to run or be trans.
Whose body do I maneuver when the deer inside me darts wildly?
If this poem was an arrow in its prey, it'd be my only candle in the dark.

If only I'd been given a woman's curves I'd know
if ghosts ask for permission when deserting the body.
If this poem was a new body I'd sing every day;
if it weren't for the wounded deer I've become, I'd run wild.

Boy with the Blue Nails

there is a boy that moves to music on stage
who's all smile and teeth,

whose eyes meet any spotlight
and he be all giddy and hood.

words rap with any note
the wind drop, be it dust or water,

he twirls and shoots arms to the air saying:
god i am yours, he punches and pulls the air,

but not before I am mine. with nail polished fingers
tucked in a fist he swivels his lower half

with dashing steps to the edge of the stage,
pirouettes, and strikes lightning at my boy heart.

when they ask me what music is
i be like: his body and any loose leaves

that hold on to their branch through winter.
spring blooms from his dance steps while

the top half of his body be all wings
and sun dios and Iztaccíhuatl about his dance.

there is something about migration—the way his body
collapses inward into the sun in his belly searching for food—

he be like that, a citizen of any country that play music con ritmo—
it's the only way he eats. when the beat drop or soften like leaf whistle

out swirl his arms to the sky like green vines
or "ayudames" or "love me,"

but the flower in his palms always blooms full and bright
without backtracking unless it's part of the song.

he rap through the dancing or wrap his body round the words,
there is no difference in his coming.

when you see a boy dance, surrender
the confines of what kind of man, you'll force him to be;

swerve your own body with each of his curves. be led.
his fingers be beating heart so hold them, man,

he don't let the music escape him during the final act,
reaches to hold,

each move a command for wind to stay under
his feathers, a kiss before goodbye.

dive deep into a light only found deep in the earth
and you'll find a boy dancing there all

mud child, core, dangling crystals from his ears—
boy, all gold chain and nail polish and shit—

he will be humming and moving like prophet in a womb.
there is a brown boy that dances in front of the burst of creation.

all star, no stage afterall, but all eyes on him anyways
and he'll stay rapping in the quiet of space

stay rapping stay stay rapping and he'll say,
i'll see you in the summertime, see you in the wintertime

and just like that the boy heart in me be reborn
fully aware of what kind of god to pray to.

Ways of Dating

Pupils
caress the surface of the sleepy honey jar and the white curtain his mother gave you

mundanely
billowing at noon. 18 hours of wide-eyed scrolling his texts and you hear

God
speak in a clear sentence, *DUMP HIS ASS. He never did anything for you anyways!* You

question
your own palmistry and doubt your fortune teller has anything good to say tonight, but

he
is *still* your lover, yet there is no name for what you both have become.

Glass,
you'll remember from a recent Google search, should actually be called Liquid

Sand
Molded and Pressured in a Furnace. Tonight, he won't call you

Honey,
after you confront the unknown names in his phone. It is then you understand why your

curtains
are not referred to as: Myriad of White Lifelines, Cotton

Coddling
Itself Skinny Sewed and Weaved Many, Many Times. The word Curtains is easier to burn.

Glass,
easier to shatter. Why do we stubbornly misname the truth and swallow?

He
will have the audacity to ask you for chamomile tea, still wet after his shower.

You
will dissolve honey in it praying that for once honey be called by its name: Swarm of

Bees,
so that by morning, Stung, is the only name he responds to.

Hood Rat

You are unseen in the ways of a shrieking rat
in a closet in a NYC apartment during a violet summer

humid with a lover who refuses to stop your misery.
Suffocate me in a trash bag or wham me with a broom,

but do something. Don't ignore my suffering!

There is a point when you surrender into the black muck,
stop lifting your trembling hairy thighs and tiny fists.

You fume an eviction with the only political power you got:
your dead stench, because smell lives forever in memory.

I ain't got nothing to prove about love—
I didn't create it anyways, so do not blame me.

The curtain in the NYC apartment billows
with the crack of a window and the bedside

penny filled glass jar will forget its weight and let
itself shatter into rolling coins and spinning shards,

round your plastic casket and even after you die
your lover won't sleep because they're too scared to kill you.

Even when your name is forgotten
you'll be teaching the world a lot about the ways of love.

Love Me the Way I Need You To

sliding wet into me, apresurado,   cognizant

of an incomplete order of events, Loud Man
questioned why my thighs felt asphyxiated in dirty sheets.

is Loud Man's muscles made from the many closets he's
lied about coming out of? i still love you.

what about the doors i closed and said don't   open,
but Loud Man punched a hole through anyways and unlocked me?

what does the dust left behind say to the key at dusk?
para no verme ridículo,

i called every threshold of his body a refuge.
how did Loud Man deport a part of me out of   my body?

when i whispered, *no quiero ahora,*
a second time

my big frail body that hasn't told his *Apa* about
the many men that led me here would do anything to be loved.

para quedar bien, i took his belt off.
dropped his jeans to the floor and let his chest hair breath me.

i said,
i said, "nevermind,"   "stop."

Loud Man conjured a brown cloud of moaning, swallowed my name
that night.

the clap of bodies gripped my flesh into curl. the   red
cross on Loud Man's wall dropped with a cold fever.

it's been years, but i have been meaning to tell you
cuartos llenos de hombres antes que tu

me trajieron a este momento. so many of my   nahs or nos
have been muffled by your enfermedad.   Loud Man, my love, you are

sick, but come here i'll hold you.
have i ever told you?

i liked you at the beginning, red roses in hand, when you
didn't interrupt what my mouth was for.

i liked you before you enlarged yourself into a man.

Sonnet With No Sound

i could turn into a million doves,
flock out of your passenger seat window,
never tell you
how much i want you to be my man, yet

i can as easily turn into volcanic rock
excavated from a mayan burial
site and be tossed behind a pyramid, left
unopened because i'm hollow. i'm silent next to you.

i don't know where i learned that mercury
in a thermostat under my tongue could kill
a baby if consumed. how has it saved so
many lives, how does it measure desire in the body.

why can't i tell you how you inflame me
in the best ways possible, yet I don't burn?

◆

how do you separate one decision into three
cardboard boxes. how do you fit:
an amorous bull, a tempestuous ocean, and a sad lion
without losing the life of each part of a choice?

sometimes i have trouble distinguishing gut-crushing
fear from random sentences like: "ask me to be your partner, like,
why is it so hard? do you wanna be my man? like my boo thang?"
should i just leave discernment to god?

how do i know i love you if it's only been three
months. what does it mean to love untethered, even while
the clock makes us older. what do i trust between the ocean water
welled in my throat,

the sad lion submissive to its cage, and the amorous
bull staring at you, my matador, not waving a red flag?

♦

the chime of war rings loudly
behind your eyes you
know how to move without saying i love you.
i am left with a single question beyond the fray.

a thousand men have died inside me.
the tongue seeks to remind you, i know war too.
their mouths open for water or an answer.
a hooked storm chills in the lung, don't speak.

we don't know how to wipe the war
from our faces, how to be each other's and safe.
both the church bell at noon and the far off lightning
strike of a thousand canons, and still we want,

we want. the three bullets of the word *yes* ring,
gunpowder when we think of being each other's boo.

Criatura Folklore

a bundle of thorn covered vines slither behind her clavicle at dawn to wake her.
some may call her   morning dew or   beast that once was, yet many

more refer to her as a warm nest for unoccupied animal bodies or boygirl.   she is a
cloaked shaman or a bare   fanged night, an exotic bird   made of fire, ash its only

trace. she is a man, the remains of an atom forced to fill the skin of dead things.
the marrow of every broken bone turns gold when she   slips in their remains.

there is no science in her hood,   no reason why coiled snakes live inside her
bowels.   readers have many questions regarding her body because she never had one.

there is no way to measure the claw marks, chicken talons, red heels, or marveling eyes
in her. how does she explain her testes   hurt when her pelvis is a slug coiled with its lover

from a branch? her breasts blend into the musculature of a wild stallion   under a full moon, no
return to last night's serpentine dress the morning after.   she is a child face, a girlboy with full

black eyes—a newborn blue bull still attached to its mother,
or a black bear worth its price in blood and a hunter's senile smile. sometimes

she feels like nothing.

sliding into the sleeve of her blazer before work   she shrinks her arm into a
flying fish,   sinks deep into a blue place plastic nets can't reach. on most days

a lover can't hold her three dimensions,   her edges, or her lost tumbleweed
hair.   wherever she goes she is foreign.   how daunting,

even wild boy skeletons fret being her.   even animal skeletons fear loving her.
she is luminescent rarity, she is,   and she never drowned

children or roamed the desert alone, i promise.   some say
her wings slurp into her shoulder blades to hide the fury   on date nights.

womanboy,   bear or sly harpy growling, hungry, all at once. some   have
seen her,   passport clutched in acrylic nails.   she doesn't have an origin

story, but everyone can smell her black wings.   it is not burnt lavender or
pepper,   it is the perfume of minced fuschias in a little girl's

hands by the river   watching her brother pick a river stone and hold it to his
little boy chest.   some say   she is open   raw in ways only devoured

animals can be   others say she is the face of darkness   tangled
talons,   scale, mane,   yellow eyes,   a chimera warring invaders with the softest melody,

while working a full time job.   regardless of what they say, i promise you, she's all
bad bitch and the reason matter shoves her into   all living things.

Reason Men Build Walls

My lover fears me.

There is too much cumbia,
        too much Selena in my walk.

        Too much Frank Ocean in my lovin',
                too much storm in our summer kiss.

I am too-much-sugar-pyramid on his tongue,
        too-much-Holy-Spirit, too many ancestors

        talking in a crowded room.
           My lover fears me:

he only sees threat in my soil-brown
        eyes: a pending earthquake,

        a possession or a steep cliff, his imminent dive out the closet.
           He fears the nature of my wild harvest,

the way I am hard fruit cracked open, soft
        inside, and his body drools.

        He is not used to the howling woman on the tip of my tongue,
           not used to myth being truth.

Of course I'm a threat. My pulping heart is a caution
        sign, a red light he dare not cross because

        he is not a man used to the elements,
           the ways of the Earth:

the way my love like fire ignites a forest;
        my presence lifts him between

his thighs like wind does dust—
        he is not used to a transient, borderless caress

like sound bath or universe energy cascading onto
        cranium, jolting him into dance with me in bed

        past nirvana and all of God's children.
            He is a coward—a divide that swore

it would let me travel across its height without papeles.

My lover is a conditioned man since the start of time,
        a colonizer that fears the Pi'ma Indian

        in me, the eagle, the flight, the ritual of me.
            He fears the too-bare earth-child, the savage,

the Tarahumara in me, fears the too-bare lepe in me:
        the too-masculine, female coalescence that makes me a god:

        the healer and warrior in me.

He tried to sever parts of me during his inner war:
        tried to slice me with his love like a molten silver sword,

        he tried to fling my soft womb inflamed into abyss,
            but with my too-much-bidi-bidi-bom-bom in my hip,

too-much-Frank-Ocean in my lovin',
        being too-much-divine and storm in the summer,

        being too good of a serpentine shapeshifter,
            I dodged and shattered a fragile masculinity.

        I, the two spirit beast, am the reason why men build

walls, borders on their fingertips. I am the catalyst for why
        men don't shed tears, don't open up.

        To lovers I will always be a wild criatura, danger, a disease,
            a howling spirit, a haunted house,

awakening, awakening, awakening

and God forbid I awaken a man in our era of silence and crosses.
      Yet, although the man that swore he loved me left runnin',

          abandoned me, wings outstretched, crown in hand,
                I hair-flipped knowing that silence

is the only way men will ever know how to love
      because a freedom like me exists.

Dressing Myself Mami

this song is not an analogy about mami's
miscarriage

it's not about her guilt working strenuous
hours leaving me with grammar equations alone

this unresolved-story is not about the man she wept for that
left us in a foreign country   alone without syntactic

competency for a new language or dinero

this prophecy is not about her clinic abortion after the wind
mysteriously left her impregnated with my father's second child

i had to do it amor i couldn't take care of
you and your brother   and me and   me

in a new country all alone

this proclamation is about how i pretend
myself to be a bearer of children or tatarabuela with a long line of progeny

these words are how i document the way i mourn for a rounder belly
filled with a zygote who will   live

and become toddler who will fill the walls of my home with laughter
and scribbles on the floor that say   *i love you mami*

these couplets are about my uterus
walls how they open and i glide out—how every full

moon is a perpetual flushing that won't come back—
me   slipping   from   me

sometimes i wish i could conjure my dreams
into reality the same way i write stories—

if i could i would script a uterus to glow towards me
halo singing angels and all—

how i would reach for it and stuff it
into my chest and

believe in god again—from my chest
children would fly out like doves the crowd would weep

at my coming this obituary is about how i want to be a mother
but a whole body is at war with me

pero aun i don't know a formula
to make me a better daughter though—

what a sinister balk i am to unbury all of mami's secrets
to create a telenovela out of the trauma she suffered simply

to immortalize us in a country that never wanted us
remembered in the fabric of its history

maybe i want to carry the bricks lumped on her shoulders
to know what it's like to be a house a mother anything but

a male-bodied cage

i wear her heartbreak use her red lipstick and outline
my eyes with black wings like i'm not already a funeral

all on my own wishing i was wishing i was woman enough
i'll never be an *ama* never be woman enough only an   aside

but even on my loneliest nights singing the songs of the mothers before me
even when i steal from my own mother without citation

she places her arms around my broad shoulders and with a wide
smile on her face says

mi vida, everything that's mine
has always been yours—

including the woman inside of you

Feathered Serpiente

There is an ancient woman dug beneath the rubble—
    my immigrant male body.

      She pushes against my mestizo pelvis, her coffin
        door, to rise from her grave every morning.

          She tickles my tongue avidly finding puertas
            to snicker or howl her way out of me.

               My father doesn't know I'm his daughter too.
                 He doesn't know how the single woman in me

                    has built a village. This woman wants
                 my father to see the tiny women she's trained

             for war even at the expense of them dying unseen.
          She is an herbalist, a sabia that pulls

         trees from seeds and boils herbs that cure
      ineptitude. She is the soldier who prepares

     the women in me to carry guns in arms
   instead of men. She is an Ancient Diosa

under daylight and a feminine vulture at dusk.
    She is wide-eyed, brown, thick and big-lipped,

      the tones of indigeneity. She sits at her temple,
        wings tucked in while the tiny women pray.

          These women don't sleep to uphold my uterus
            in the air as if it were a God in need of holding.

             They fold prayers into my womb to keep it alive.
               They submerge me in ocean water during dysphoric

endless nights. These women trail the streets singing,
candles lit, and scripts unfurled to clutch me when I fall

out of my skin.

Mother deity soars down from the furthest sun,
holds a mirror to my face, the landscape of tired rubble she sees

doesn't suit this moon queen. So she holds a razor in claw,
shaves feverishly to deny man the power that has caged her.

Her beak opens to a roar, wears blood-red lipstick, re-writes
bibles, honors her tiny brown women with feathered crown pieces.

Wild-haired, she dives for me wings outstretched and
proclaims her victory in this war.

My body is her body.

All cross-legged in the temple, chalk in hand against blackboard,
the crowned women solve the mystery of how

I got stuck in this body and how the hell
I'm going to tell my father I'm his daughter too.

Sunset in Chihuahua

Little Boy walks up a rail-less
flight of stairs to the cement
flat roof of Father's house. Father, in black
scorpion-skinned boots, follows.

That one, Father points to a brick,
is going to be your room.
He points to the Mexican sky and takes a sip of
beer to withhold any more promises.

From atop, Little Boy looks out across cement
town below: dirt roads, green roosters, naked children—
Little Boy snaps a picture with a blink and not
his Polaroid camera. He wants to forget. Father is

lying again.

Little Boy wants the road dirt etched on his stomach
to remember something he never lived.
Instead of dad-hood Father tips cowboy hat and
offers brick as home, so Little Boy remains air unclaimed.

The story of them is complicated,
yet Father continues tangling it: That one right there,
he points to a slithering, albino
snake, will be your sister and brother's room.

Father never says "half-siblings" or
owns his "half-of-the-problem," Little Boy
thinks, but still he nods in the kind of interest
you give an old man with a cowboy hat that is

dying.
Father says, I think I'll install the sink
here, and points to his chest. Little Boy looks
at the carcass of cement, the unfinished bones of a second

story Father will never build. Little Boy
tucks his hands in his jean jacket, sets his marble eyes on the blood
orange desert land that will never fit in his pocket. He is not Little Boy.
He is Man visiting Father after 20 years, but it feels the same.

Man looks at Father. Man shuts close his faucet
so tears won't leave evidence of forgiveness, but he forgives
Father anyways for leaving Man across the border fatherless
when he was Little Boy.

♦

On purple nights Man sees Father sitting in the rib
cage of a second story house in dreams—a recurring dream:
a shadow crawls over Father's hands, while a green rooster
with the moon for its eye caws before stabbing its red beak

in a jittering albino snake. Father's wet beer bottle
slips from his hand and shatters on a brick. The black scorpion skin of his cowboy boots consumes
Father's sun-kissed flesh and grips him by the neck. The snap and twist of limbs
crumple the dream and the sweet song of a child across the desert valley lulls.

Notes

"Dontcomeformyhood":
    This poem's form was inspired by Albert Park's "Preference."

"first real nation of nations":
    This poem was inspired by Danez Smith's "my president"

"Retrato in Names":
    This poem was inspired by Ocean Vuong's "On Earth We're Briefly Gorgeous"

"(un)Documented: Answers I (Didn't) Give USCIS":
    This poem takes after Jan-Henry Gray's "I-797C Notice of Action"

"Brunch":
    This poem takes after Madison Johnson's "Actually, Yes, Everything is about Race"

"My People":
    This poem takes after Fatimah Asghar's "If They Should Come for Us"

"Ways of Dating":
    This poem was inspired by Jess X. Snow's "The Last Words of the Honey Bees"

TenQú

Telephone lines & palm trees. Marina & Angelina. The garage on Spruce & Cedar. Mami, por crear nuestra posibilidad de existir. 98th Street. Virginia Torres y Miguel Lorenzana, mis abuelitos. Tia Patty Tio Martin, my second parents, Susie Nana, my sisters—thank you for being our first country & home. Ms. Flowers. Chocomil. Don Chepo & Maricela. Tia Carmen. Mrs. Schuricht. Golden Souljahs. Pacific Theaters. Brittany Barker. Kelso & Inglewood, the center of my happiness. Sushi Sumo (before it got expensive). To all my friends that watched me perform the same poems for years. TT. Harlem & that bomb ass salad joint across the street. Eily, thanks for always being a real homie. KB Toys. Yvette Moreno, my big sister, I love you. Ballet Folclorico. Joaquina. Octavia Butler. Throat Queens. Monica Fortiz, for bomb pancakes. Steve, broski, broham, thank you for loving me. Richard Villegas Jr., I will write many novels, I promise. Laundromat on El Segundo. Madera, Chihuahua. SZA. Xavier, Havi, for taking me in broken. Los Lorenzanas. Hot Pockets. Star Donut. One Piece. Angela Davis. The Ratchet Scale (2-15). Tio Beto, "Hay Güey!" Marcos Nieves, Pea, Wil, thank you for bringing to life Serpent Goddess. Lara, oh Lara, & Mingle's Tea Bar. Mika Roque. Sentinel Field track and bleachers. Thich Nhat Hahn. Marcelo Hernandez Castillo, for believing in me. Jose Luis de la O. X-Men. Mi pasaporte Méxicano. Mr. Helenius. Ensalada de Atun. Kyoto. Isis Avalos, for giving me the movement to break free into the woman I am. The Fonsecas for taking me in as kin & calling me El Super Bebe. Mami's bomb palomas. Lalo & Pieces. Crystal Caines. Aubrianna Crystal Natalie. Audrie Lorde. Angel Hermes Eliot. Inglewood Public Library. Marietta Colar. Aaliyah Mcintosh. Rachel Resnik. Esquites. Third Degree Step Team. Elva Gomez, por siempre estar en nuestras vidas. Emah, solace & "we process the same!" Mike, for bringing to life my artwork on my skin. Yosimar Reyes, for giving me a place to belong when others didn't. Don Lee Farm. Mooji. Jabari, my baby. Fraccionamiento Francisco I. Madero Mitla 5313. Sevilla. Digimon Toys. Bowl Thai. Shared naranjas. Mr. Lewis. Mama Maiz. Professor Philogene. Shireen Justin Jayshell. Shared toronjas. Angeru. Momo. Andrew Nance, for helping me put out my first chapbook. Abraham Marquéz. Jordi, for being my alien sibling. Sailor Moon. Ramona, Maria. Yadira Miko Victor. Neptune. Brian Baab. My Mars in Cancer, CUZ. Cynthia Guardado. Nakajima Library. Crozier Middle School. Francis. Palms Up Academy. Cuahtemoc. Cardcaptor Sakura. Chihuahua, Chihuahua for being the epicenter of my first breath. Marilou Danielle Arnisha Leslie. Hollywood Park Casino. Century Community Charter School. Los Torres. Jose Manuel Lorenzana Villalvazo. Oak Street. Kelso Market. Antonio Lopez. My students, my students, my students, this is for you. Toni Morrison. Massaman Curry. Xochitl-Julisa Bermejo. Miguel Martinez. GameCube. Bannister. Social Justice House. Patricia Smith, Momma, for seeing my ugly in gold. Mode, big sis, MDLC, I love you so much, b. Carl's Jr. on Inglewood and Manchester. Centinela Park. Pi'ma & Tarahumara ancestors, I walk with you. Tio Miguel. Reyna, my Sailor Saturn. Camila Concepción, we will still write for TV, I promise. Kimberly & Emmily. DP. Posse Scholarship & my Posse. Alyesha Wise and Matthew Cuban for taking me in. Cielo, for seeing me. Tia Sandra y Tio Jose Luis. My Seeds of Liberacion. Ravard. 2018 Queer Writers of Color Cohort, ya'll know who you are. Brianna Samyra Telicia. Heart Storms. Missy Fuego. Liza, my twin. Christopher Soto. Naruto. Yesse. Da'Venar. Abuelo Ramon. Wood tipped Black & Milds. Joselyn Natalie Evelin. Queer Obsidian. Julian Sambrano, Happy by Nao minute 1:57. Sup G, Students up to Good. Leslie Guardado, twin. Lorenzana Services (Inc.). Chunky Melendez. Yellow, blue-wheeled Nickel Board. Ezak & Jovan, for seeing me. Gameboy Advance. Ashley Davis. Tsubasa Reservoir Chronicle. eXiled Poetry Society. Tanya Dre Majik. Treinta y Una & all the $3.00 I lost. Arianna Basco. Anáhuac. Vivianna Elle Nusca Moreno. Betty Arelly Cecy. Ant & Apple. Kali Fajardo—Anstine. Pokémon. Villafan. Professor Johnson. Thank you for introducing me to The Rails, my sacred home, Anah, & for loving me since the beginning of time. Maple Street. Leilani, my sister. Consuelo & Leopoldo 1. Fir Street. Yazmin Monet. Korra. Kryss. Nikki, Nikkilandia, for holding it down for me all the time. Mi Torito. Z. Jasmine Julissa Stevie. ING Fellowship. Armando Garcia, for always showing up. LAX Tacos. Eduardo Brenda Jose Luisito. Bates Sensei. Monica Carranza for creating order out of my poems. Michaé, for seeing me. Alma Ramirez. Jorge, Dulce, Marisol, & Ricky. City Walk. Juan Carlos, for giving us freedom. Food For Thought Open Mic. Yuko Shimomoto. Ms. Meyers. A.H. or Puppycat. Justin Portia Ebony. Mrs. Means & Mrs. Garcia. Beatboxing Ying Yang twins, life partner, Janboogie, Janette, my love, thank you for seeing & holding me. Ms. Joo. Leopoldo 2, apa. The Vortex. Eddy, my love. Juanita, love is waiting for you. Loteria. Sundress Publications. Frank Ocean. Erin Smith. Eduardo's Barber Shop. Tierney. Queer Obsidian. Domo. My beloved literary agent & dearest sister, Janel Pineda. Our unborn children, playing in a jungle gym in the sky. Best Bargain. Bougainvillea. Elly. Santa Muerte Tarot Deck. Bamby Salcedo. The first album of Panic! At the Disco. Adan & Hiro. Michelle Gutierrez. Nintendo Switch. The Eagles' Hotel California. Mayi, Ismael Jimenez, my first student, this is for you. Mami, por ser el principio y el fin de esta historia. Te amo hasta El Cielo del Casino, mi alcornoque.

& to my readers, thank you for holding my first-born by the hand. May this book make you laugh, hold you if you need it, & give you a place to exist, reflect, love, & challenge life as it is.

About the Author

féi iká shumarí (b.1993, Chihuahua, Mexico) is a 2 Spirit/trans woman, (un)documented writer, performance artist, and graphic designer. She is a 2023 Lambda Literary fellow and 2022 Tin House Scholar. féi is the author of HOOD CRIATURA (Sundress Publications, 2020), the forthcoming CHABÓCHI DOLL (Abode Press, 2026) and (UN)DOCU MENTE (Noemi Press, 2027). féi's poetry/ prose is published in *Los Angeles Review of Books*, *POETRY*, *Academy of American Poets*, *Hayden Ferry's Review*, *Oxford Review of Books*, *TransLash Media*, *Somewhere we are Human* (Harper Collins, 2022), *Here to Stay* (Harper Collins, 2024), *Split This Rock*, *F News Magazine*, and more. féi is a descendent of the Pi'ma, Rarámuri, and Cora peoples. To stay up to date with her writing subscribe to feiikashumari.substack.com. For more of her projects, designs, services and products visit feiikashumari.com.

Other Sundress Titles

nightsong
Ever Jones
$16

JAW
Albert Abonado
$16

Bury Me in Thunder
moira j.
$16

Gender Flytrap
Zoë Estelle Hitzel
$16

Boom Box
Amorak Huey
$16

Afakasi | Half-Caste
Hali F. Sofala-Jones
$16

Match Cut
Letitia Trent
$16

Divining Bones
Charlie Bondus
$16

Maps of Injury
Chera Hammons
$16

Lessons in Breathing Underwater
HK Hummel
$16

Dead Man's Float
Ruth Foley
$16

Blood Stripes
Aaron Graham
$16

Arabilis
Leah Silvieus
$16

Marvels
MR Sheffield
$20

Passing Through Humansville
Karen Craigo
$16

Phantom Tongue
Steven Sanchez
$15

www.ingramcontent.com/pod-product-compliance
Lightning Source LLC
Chambersburg PA
CBHW081419090426
42738CB00017B/3422